THE
TRASH MEN
OF
WAR

HARRY BAGWANDEEN

Daisa
PUBLISHING

THE TRASH MEN OF WAR
First published in Great Britain in 2020 by
DAISA PUBLISHING
An imprint of PARTNERSHIP PUBLISHING

Written by Harry Bagwandeen
Copyright © Harry Bagwandeen 2020
Photography © by Harry Bagwandeen 2020

A CIP catalogue record for this book is available from the British Library.

ISBN 978-1-9162251-8-3
eBook ISBN 978-1-9162251-7-6

Book cover design by: Partnership Publishing

Book typeset by:
PARTNERSHIP PUBLISHING
Barton upon Humber
North Lincolnshire
United Kingdom
DN18 5RG

www.partnershippublishing.co.uk

Printed in England

Partnership Publishing is committed to a sustainable future for our business, our readers, and our
planet; an organisation dedicated to promoting responsible management of forest resources.

This book is made from paper certified by the Forestry Stewardship Council (FSC) an
organisation dedicated to promoting responsible management of forest resources.

DEDICATION

This book is in memory of a courageous and great
friend, Neil Sprankle.

Neil sadly died in 2011 in a fireworks accident aged 25
with four other colleagues in Hawaii.

To the security teams who risked their lives and to the
ones that lost theirs in Iraq keeping me safe ...

Thank you all, I am forever indebted to you.

Due to personal circumstances, I was offered a position in Iraq which I enthusiastically accepted.

The Trash Men of War
is my account of this amazing adventure …

CONTENTS

ANOTHER NEW BEGINNING

My lifelong interest in weapons and things that go bang started in 1970 at the tender age of four when I was allowed to use my big brother's pellet gun. I was even on the receiving end once or twice … It really hurt! By the age of eight, I had graduated to my father's 12-gauge shotgun, trips to the bottom field for pigeon shooting with Dad were a regular occurrence before going to primary school.

Around the inquisitive age of ten, I was a bit of an experimenter and with my chemistry set, I wondered what would happen if I filled a small glass tube with toy gun caps, seal it at both ends with some glue and with a length of wire, hold it in the flame of the methylated spirit burner to see what would happen. It took a while to see what the result would be due to the tube bouncing about, in and out of the flame. I did eventually get my result - a small CRACK!

In the blink of an eye, the tube had disappeared.

A few seconds later I felt spots of sharp pain in my hands and face; unsurprisingly they contained small bits of shattered glass. I removed the bits from my hands but I didn't know what state my face was in, which meant going to see a grown up … my big sister.

'I'm in trouble now', I thought. My sister spent some time picking bits of glass out my face. I don't really know what I was expecting to happen but felt relieved that I could still see.

I was thirteen before I decided upon numerous other experiments. One was a homemade cannon; a thin copper tube squeezed flat at one end to seal it and a tiny hole in a sealed portion for an ignition hole, half filled with matches. I used a vice, squeezed the matches tight into the tube with a small rod to almost half their original volume. The rod that I used for the squeeze was in too tightly, so I'd give it a twist.

This was not a great idea! The bang was deafening and sounded like a shot gun going off. I had almost blown my thumb off and burned the next two fingers! I was taken to hospital where the receptionist said one thing, "It's true what they say about matches." Point taken.

So I moved on to making gunpowder … I had never heard anyone say, 'don't play around with gunpowder'.

I got the recipe from some 1963 encyclopaedias we had at home. I remember reading something about rockets, that they never thought man would ever reach the moon!

After getting all the ingredients and the approximate proportions, I started burning holes in things here and there. If only I knew then what I know now, I would probably have had better results. I was hooked! I decided that it would be beneficial to take up chemistry as I had been told by an older student that they made TNT in sixth form!

-

I did a spell in the RAF as an armourer for guns, bombs, bullets and then I found out that the RAF had its own full time EOD (Explosives Ordnance Disposal) unit. After several applications, I was there for 3 ½ years.

It was my dream job, something I always wanted to do. I was nineteen and I had a great time.

After leaving the Air Force, I did a number of jobs from; washing up in restaurants, boat propeller finisher, some factory work and 3 years training and working as an acupuncturist, amongst others. It would be over 20 years before I finally got my bomb disposal certificate. Proof was essential before I could go to Iraq.

In 2004 I added another string to my bow, I had just qualified as a dental technician and was working in one of the most prestigious medical addresses in the world, Harley Street in London. I loved the work and the people, my boss was and still is a good friend and I try to visit him every time I am in town. I just got a real buzz from working in London but I decided that because I had internet and out of sheer curiosity, I'd see what EOD jobs, if any, were available.

I came up trumps and then I was given the opportunity to resume my EOD career by a UK company. This mainly consisted of standing and wandering around muddy, freezing cold building sites in London, looking into holes for anything cylindrical, as most ordnance is, or just waiting for a call from one of the site workers. Not the most glorious of jobs, but a lot less stressful than being a dental technician. There were one or two jobs which had alternative benefits.

One consisted of being on standby while some marine engineers repaired groynes on Shoeburyness Beach, which was and still is used as an ammunition testing ground.

This entailed working with the tide, being on the beach, collecting and eating oysters and digging for bait worms and investigating the odd bit of ordnance that was discovered.

When the tide came in, out came everyone's rods for the summer bass which were pretty bountiful and tasty.

Another job in Cambridgeshire consisted of checking an area prior to archaeologists doing their thing, as it was a site of valuable interest. It had been a former RAF base, so runways and perimeter tracks were still in place.

The majority of disposalers have all been in the military, and as a consequence seem to like guns, rifles, ordnance and of course, shooting. The site was full of game and quarry, a quick word with the farmers and an unofficial 'OK' was given. After the first week about seven air rifles appeared. There were only five people staying on the site, this offered some extra site security. I had a soft-top car, so with the roof down, someone would drive around the perimeter track, another would crouch in the passenger seat and call a stop, and another rabbit would be bagged. We ended up buying a slow cooker and with all the bagged quarry always on the go, we decided to call it 'Oakington Stew' … yum.

On another occasion due to there being some rare wildlife on the site, we had a number of ecologists working for their protection. One of them was heard to comment that he 'liked hare'.

One Friday morning just before embarking on a job in London for the week, I thought I would bag one for his weekend meal. This was done, all prepared ready for the pot. When it was presented to him, like a prize.

"What's this?" he asked, confused.

"Hare," was the reply. "You like hare!"

"Yes, I like watching them in the field!"

-

2006 was a particularly emotional time for me; my marriage wasn't working and I was quite in debt. I decided on trying to save the former, so I left my job as it meant being away all week, but not knowing what to do, I was considering some factory work after sending out many résumés, with no replies.

Then one day out of the blue, I got a phone call.

"Want to go to Iraq?"

Almost before the question was even finished and without really thinking of the consequences, "Yes please." I replied.

I thought at least I would get myself out of debt and take some of the strain off my wife. I had always said to myself, 'Iraq? Never, sounds far too dangerous for me'. At the time, it was being reported every day on the BBC, so many military coalition and contractors were dying and it played heavily on my mind, but I didn't have much choice.

FORT BLISS, EL PASO, TEXAS

Within a few weeks I was off to El Paso which I had only ever heard about in westerns and didn't really know where it was. Texas - that's where it was and still is to my knowledge. There I got my briefing, uniform, inoculations, a gasmask, body armour and helmet; all courtesy of the US Government. So I had a small, all expenses paid holiday; a week in the US in El Paso, somewhere I never thought I'd go to. Great, as I love to travel. I was given loads of free stuff, teeth checked, flu shot, HIV test and a clean bill of health before heading off into the unknown.

On leaving the States there were now six UXO (Unexploded Ordnance) technicians; five Brits and an ex American Ranger called Rick. We met Rick in El Paso at Fort Bliss; he was a hard, sort of *Hells' Angel* looking bloke with a really dry sense of humour, he always had his arms folded, sunglasses on and never smiled at the minions.

We had a stopover in London for a number of hours, long enough to meet my wife, we only lived 45 minutes away. She treated us all to lunch at the OXO Tower, a salubrious restaurant on the South Bank of the River Thames. I guess it was a sort of going away present and a nice thing to do.

After lunch, we went on a whirlwind sightseeing tour of London, a few pictures by Big Ben, topped off by a trip to Harrods for those who hadn't been to London before; I think there was more than one.

On leaving Harrods, it was time to say goodbye to my wife, which was a little bit more difficult than I had expected. We kissed and had a longer than usual cuddle at the entrance to the underground. I felt physically numb but tried not to show it, we said our goodbyes as I descended down the steps into the darkness of the tube station. Halfway down the steps I glanced back, her long black coat and her pink cashmere scarf, with an almost blank expression on her face, there was no smile. I looked back, holding the image of my wife, framed in the grey light of day. As I turned away from her, my eyes immediately started to well up. I hoped not, but this could very well be the last time I saw her.

I was emotionally stunned, choked up and could barely speak all the way to Heathrow. All I could think about was her and I had resigned myself that I wouldn't see her again. It felt like I was going on a suicide mission; if I survived, it would be a real bonus.

Letting off some steam, I enjoyed a few beers later with the lads at the airport, my thoughts started working overtime on my wife, who I might have seen for the last time.

'What was to come and how was it going to end'?

OUR LAST SUPPER

Our next stop from London was Kuwait City, then a 30-minute drive to Ali Al Salem Airbase. This was the transit point for all the military and civilians going into Iraq. Everything was hot and sand coloured.

The first stop on arrival to the airbase was to collect our bedding, together with our 70lbs plus of kit that we had acquired in the States. We then traipsed through the sand, passed rows and rows of sand coloured tents in alphanumeric order. We eventually found ours which was N1, right at the front, through a squeaky wooden door and then some plastic screening.

Inside was full of double bunks and there was a huge material tube with flap-covered holes running down the centre of the roof. This was the air conditioning distributor connected to a unit outside the tent.

We grabbed whichever bunk was free but the top one was best as it was nearer to the aircon. The toilets, shower and laundry blocks were on the periphery of the rows of tents. The toilets were a great source of amusement and meant visiting all the stalls; always spending a few minutes longer than necessary reading all the graffiti, the majority consisted of Chuck Norris jokes, lots about accommodating wives and girlfriends, and various unit company commanders.

The tent was only a short walk from the air terminal, we were all going to different places, but some were going to the same place as myself. I think it took almost four days before I finally got a flight out. Checking the flight manifesto to see if I was on a Baghdad flight, 6am, 10am, 3pm, 7pm, 2am. I thought this was some kind of test to see if we could stay awake for days at a time! During my time there, I felt quite at ease, as this part of the Middle East was safe- there were no insurgents or fighting here, but I would be leaving soon; what would happen on the next part of my journey?

My apprehension was almost palpable.

On arrival in Baghdad, I anticipated scenes not dissimilar from all those Vietnam war films I had seen but a bit more modern and with a Middle Eastern flavour to it. How wrong I was. Food was the biggest shock and as they say an army marches on its stomach, and how right that is. There was a KFC, Popeye Chicken, Pizza Hut and a vast array of branded coffee shops.

TAKE AWAY ANYONE?

Shops that sold everything from tax free designer sunglasses to the newest and greatest, blackest multi-tools, computers, and the latest Xbox game.

The food in the numerous cook houses offered everything you could possibly want to eat which was eaten off either segmented plastic or paper plates with plastic cutlery to save on washing up. Water is pretty precious and comes at a premium in the desert.

The plastic forks always snapped when they came within an inch of anything harder than a fried egg. I remedied this problem on my return from my first leave and a lovely British Airways stewardess supplied me with a full metal set of cutlery from business class which I still have. The cook houses had almost every soft drink on the market and some more.

On one visit to the cookhouse, I was with the biker, 'Rick from the States', with whom I had travelled out with from El Paso. He was driving the truck to dinner, but both being new to Baghdad, neither of us were quite sure where to go. We stopped and asked a passing US soldier. Me being the nearest, I asked him in my best English accent, "Excuse me, can you tell me the way to the chow hall?"

He looked at me as if I just spurted a load of Martian at him and by the look on his face, I knew he didn't have a clue what I was talking about.

After a small pause, I repeated myself. This time he had almost tuned-in, but I knew he still wasn't sure if it was English, so my 'partner-in-meals' repeated exactly what I had said but in a normal American accent and the answer back was immediate. We laughed and laughed all the way to the chow hall.

People seemed to be going about their business in the normal way and could have almost been anywhere in the world. We were not; we were in a real dangerous place and the former home to the dictator, Saddam Hussein Abd al-Majid al-Tikriti. It now was occupied by the coalition military in all its force.

Behind the facade of one of Saddam's many palace complexes and all its reassigned satellite buildings, betwixt with date palm lined roads, lakes and mosques, (he even had a load of hollow conical towers built of mud with small holes in them; these were bat-roosts, supposedly to help keep the mosquitoes down), the Blackhawk helicopters were taking off and landing at regular intervals kicking up a load of dust each time they did so, scores of military vehicle convoys in their vast array of shapes and sizes also kicking up major dust clouds every time one passed.

There were concrete guard posts surrounded by sand bags and ID checks at every turn. Tall radio masts on every high point. Most of the major roads near important areas, like the airport, were lined with 'T' walls, 6 or 7 metres high, interlocking for bomb blast suppression to the more sinister covert goings-on, deciding how to stop the insurgency that was causing so much death and destruction. Whilst winning the 'hearts and minds' to gain the confidence of the Iraqi people to show them the benefits of the coalition military presence.

AND THE BAND PLAYS ON

And so, on to my first site. This entailed travelling by road in an armed convoy of probably seven or more heavily armoured vehicles and with top shooters on each. Body armour and helmet on and with all our belongings on board we left Baghdad early o'clock.

This was my first 'very real' taste of the unknown and fear as we were going into the dangerous part of Iraq and leaving the relative safety of 'Camp Victory' as it was known.

The journey was long, uneventful, hot and very uncomfortable, everyone was strapped tightly into their seats, with only a tiny offset window with two-inch thick armoured glass at knee height for light and shadows.

BAGHDAD DEPARTURE EARLY O'CLOCK

I slept most of the way, not really knowing how long the journey was going to take or if we were going to be hit by a roadside bomb.

If I was asleep, then hopefully if we did get hit I wouldn't know much about it, if it was to happen, I had 'made my bed' and would have to deal with the consequences.

We arrived up north somewhere many hours later; we had made it unscathed and relieved.

We dumped our bags off at our accommodation, this consisted of 2 rows of small huts with a concrete pathway down the middle and gravel in-between the huts and the path; I had number 5. It was a small hut with 2 doors, raised up on legs with 3 metal fabricated steps leading to the entrances. I had half of the hut, which was partitioned by a really thin wall separating the two rooms.

Inside was a desk, a bed and a wardrobe. There was a window which was blocked out by a sheet of wood for night time black out. This was 'home' for the next 9 months.

We then went for food. It was Friday, so the menu was lobster, king crab legs and steak - cooked to order.

We had a briefing as to where we were to work at a site called Arlington (13 miles away), how we were to get there, and what to do in case we got hit by a roadside bomb or had an incoming attack. They told us where the nearest shelters were, plus a few pleasantries and introductions, then it was time to unpack, shower and get to bed, ready for another early start.

We were up before the cock but not before the minarets calling the faithful to prayer from the local village. Breakfast consisted of (unheard of to the Brits anyway) stuff like grits, biscuits and gravy, non-pork bacon, wieners and eggs anyway you wanted them, as long as they were boiled.

We then had the first of many briefings. How, where, what to do, and what came to be one of my favourite and most interesting parts of every work day which was the local intelligence about what had happened the day before. Normally, several IEDs (Improvised Explosive Device), some shootings and the odd beheading were all within a few miles radius of us. In time and in a perverse sort of way, I felt quite excited by this, as it put me right in the thick of things.

I was itching to see some sort of action, to face the test of how I would ultimately cope under the auspices of death; it was a far cry from what I had left at home.

EN ROUTE TO ARLINGTON

The roads we took to work were given an American designation as were some of the work sites, the rest were honourably named after someone who had died over there. This tradition is still happening.

Most of the Iraqi road names were pretty difficult to pronounce and it also served as a simple code, so anyone listening in to the radio traffic who shouldn't have been, wouldn't have been the wiser. The transmission wouldn't have made much sense either; 'six clicks along Hershey and right on to Tampa etc'.

We arrived at the periphery of Arlington ammunition depot, through our security checkpoint, then on to the main site, this was one of Saddam's explosive storage areas and had over 80 sand-covered bunkers and 80 or so massive warehouse-type buildings covering an area of 27 square kilometres.

On passing through security we drove for about another 15 minutes down the site centre road of hard gravel until we got to the centre of operations and admin area.

The whole place was ours, we de-body armoured and had yet another brief on the day's activities. We would be separating out serviceable tank ammunition into their different roles; high explosive, anti-tank, armour-piercing and same colour boxes, putting them on pallets with the banding really straight and parallel. We had the use of about 20 local nationals (LNs) per team, there were several teams.

Also mentioned in the brief was instruction of safety when working with the locals, and the many don'ts-don't give them bottled water as they had their sterilised water from a large bladder tank, which tasted like swimming pool water only stronger.

Don't turn your back on them, don't let them go off into the bush for the toilet as they could be planting IEDs, don't let them in the front cab of your vehicle as they will cut your throat so much as look at you.

'Hmm', I thought, 'this is going to be interesting especially as they're hands-on dealing with the ammunition'.

ARLINGTON BUNKERS (SCREEN GRAB IMAGE)

On first meeting them however such was my paranoia, I was expecting to be attacked at any moment, but this turned out not to be the case. Most of them were wearing a shemagh, (an interesting and very versatile piece of cloth. It can denote tribe and standing, depending on the colour and the way it is worn. It keeps you hot when wrapped all over the face, which is much better than very hot, the sand and dust out of your lungs as it acts like a filter and if you soak it in water and hold it up wind then it works like your own personal air conditioning due to the evaporating liquid), sun glasses and pseudo shemaghs of thick woollen ski masks were worn by some …

With some of them, it was a week before I finally saw their faces. They all seemed pretty OK. Apart from the language barrier which was no fault of theirs (at the time my Arabic was non-existent), and a general lack of personal hygiene on their part!

In general they worked pretty hard in the heat, for little pay and little food but it was kind of expected from them and I think what they expected too. There were limits though and a few months into the contract, at lunch time all the LNs were driven off to an out of the way area off the main site for their lunch and being as I will eat almost anything (I draw the line at insects and just can't see the point), I would always check what they had for lunch to see if I could do the work they were doing on the food they were given.

One day it was c'hubus (large round flat bread), some red tomato water and two small pieces of potato. No way was that enough, and I complained to my supervisor.

Like so many Iraqis, the caterers just wanted the money and the more they could get away with, the less food was supplied. Within an hour the food contract was withdrawn, and a new caterer was supplied.

After a while and with everyone sizing each other up, the questions started from the locals who surprisingly could speak very good English. "What is your name Mr? Where are you from Mr? How many children Mr?" These were the standard questions and the odd one asking for toothpaste or some other essentials.

LOCAL NATIONALS

We spent a few days acclimatising to the heat. Some days were so hot, that on one occasion after having washed my hands with soap and water, so they were really wet, I walked outside whilst rubbing my wet hands together and in just a few steps they were bone dry. Now I gauge all restaurant hand-dryers by this. Again due to the extreme heat, a frozen bottle of water placed in the shade, within 20 minutes it would be hot enough to make a half decent cup of tea!

HOT!

After familiarising myself with the drills of the day's routine, I started seeking out the wildlife more and more, taking pictures at every opportunity.

There was such a diverse array of wildlife, all the mammals were sand coloured and had massive ears to aid them in keeping cool in the heat. Some really colourful birds that all went to ground every time an eagle flew overhead. There were all kinds of lizards and some scarily hairy bugs.

It isn't every day you see one of the deadliest scorpions in the world!

The locals cottoned on pretty quickly that if they brought me a weird looking praying mantis or caterpillar they could all take a five-minute break while I took some pictures of it; hoping that I wouldn't notice ... It worked quite well for both them and me.

FEEDING SCORPIAN

BUG ON A THISTLE

IN JAIL

SNAKE AND BUGS

Although this project was interesting and I loved the job, I did at times think a lot of money was being wasted. We spent a month or so preparing an ammunition shipment to be moved to another depot as Arlington was supposed to close and be handed back to the Iraqi army. The whole shipment consisted of 21 trucks over five separate convoys at a cost of $125,000 - maybe more. The ammunition all arrived at its destination without incident but on the returning empty convoys three of the vehicles were hit by IEDs and three drivers died.

On another returning convoy, one driver fell asleep at the wheel and crashed into another truck and died.

A few weeks later all the ammunition was returned to where it had started from, as the site it had been delivered to was closing down instead and this depot, being much larger was now staying open.

Apart from supervising the locals, I had acquired a new skill of driving different types of forklifts, pertinent in the job as all the pallets of ammunition needed to be transported and either re-stacked in the bunkers or warehouses or moved to a central area, known as the football field, to be further re-distributed to another part of the site from here ...

I was working with another Brit called Paul but affectionately known as 'Looney'.

He was quite a character, who had arrived a few weeks before me and the conversation went something like this…

"Hmm, a lot of ammo and stuff here."

"Aye."

"There must be a way of making a few bob out of this stuff on eBay."

"Yep, but what?"

It took a few days to come up with an idea. After seeing boxed PG9 rockets everywhere it was found that the tail fins were only screwed in and easily removed, so we decided that they would make great key fobs. That was the plan and for quite some time afterwards, two Brits were often seen at each stack with the box lids up on all the PG9 stacks.

I finally put one up on eBay three days after they hung Saddam, only to have it removed. After several discussions with eBay, I gave up and ended up giving mine out to some good people I have met since.

PG9 ROCKETS

I had now been there for some months and had settled in quite nicely. One evening, Looney and I were sat outside chatting, as you do.

It was when we started hearing some gunfire way off in the distance. We thought, 'let's go and see if we can see anything'.

We went outside of our compound although still on the base and saw a few rounds of tracer in the distance. This went on for a while, maybe ten minutes or so, then the intensity increased. We discussed how probably some insurgents were trying to gain access to the main camp and had been found out.

After another five minutes or so flares started going off illuminating the area where the shooting was coming from.

This was too good to miss, so I quickly went back to my room and got my video camera, came back and started filming. We could see more tracer ammunition, some sort of searchlight and more shooting. While we were discussing what was going on, we thought what are we doing here?

There is a firefight going on no further than a kilometre away and we were stood there, just chatting and filming it and who knew what the outcome was to be.

How blasé we had become about the whole thing; after all we could be overrun by attacking insurgents and ended up as a commemorative beer, served without a head!

I think we mentally decided that we would deal with it when we came to that bridge.

In the meantime, we would let the Army deal with the situation.

Then the activity started to die down, "anything more?"

"Nope."

"OK , I'm off to bed."

"Me too."

In the morning, I told loads of colleagues about the firefight and how insurgents were trying to get in, but they must have all been killed. In the morning's local intelligence briefing … Nothing! I asked the Security boss and he said, "No, it was just an exercise."

Everyone had their story to tell or some snippet of information they had, either on what they had been doing or seen in Iraq, and how long they had been there, some had been in the military prior and had even been fighting there. Apparently during the 80s Saddam had the third largest amount of conventional weapons in the world. One of these stories was that Saddam's chief arms buyer was given a large budget every month that he had to spend on weaponry and if he didn't then he faced execution.

Whoever he was he was pretty industrious, but some of the weapons he had bought were sub-standard and I think the countries selling them just wanted to get rid of old and defective stock.

We had one consignment of over 4.5 million 9mm pistol ammunition from Pakistan, some of which our security wanted to use for practicing with but hardly any of it worked, so really it was just a large amount of scrap which had been bought. I mention Pakistan, but during my next two years I was to see ammunition from Russia, Bulgaria, Yugoslavia, Spain, India,

Pakistan, Brazil, France, UK, USA, Germany, Yemen, Saudi Arabia, Iran, Jordan, China and Italy.

When the early-birds got there and started disposing of these arms, there were all sorts, thousands upon thousands of large high explosive air-dropped bombs, some so big that the aeroplanes that Saddam had were unable to carry them. There were also countless missiles and large rockets, and mines in their millions.

The majority of this was disposed of at Arlington and one of its claims to fame was that some of the largest ever demolition shots in the world were carried out here. True or not - I don't know.

-

Due to the extreme heat, long hours and the stress of the possibility of being blown up every day, some of the internationals were not used to this, so they would sit in their trucks with the air conditioning turned up to maximum, to supervise the locals. After lunch it was all too easy to fall asleep and several internationals were sent home, but occasionally they were just given warnings.

On one occasion our supervisor, known as 'Worm' turned up at a work site to find one asleep, he told all the locals to hide out of sight. On waking the international, he questioned, "Where are your LNs?"

"Erm, don't know."

"Time you packed your bags then, you're going home."

After working an exhausting 12 hour shift six days a week in the sun and energy zapping heat, most days we really had thought we had achieved something as we were usually hungry, covered in dust and clothes stained with sweat, and were glad to go home. Well, back to where our accommodation was, but again, we had to run the gauntlet.

After putting our armour back on, climbing into the oven of a vehicle, sweating several pints and reminding people to put their helmet on, off we went. Normally this was accompanied by some loud metal iPod track, but mostly *'Thunderstruck'* by AC/DC, I fondly recall.

If you are going to die, then this is a good track to die by!

HOME TIME

Sunday ... a day off, hooray! This normally gave us the chance to stay in bed all day, sleep or watch some hooky DVD from the local shop of the latest blockbuster movie before it was even made or the whole of the latest season of whatever. Another option on this day was to replenish toiletries or go for a real coffee at the nearest military base, about an hour away, near Tikrit and Saddam's former home and last resting place.

At that time it was a pretty dangerous place in the world to be, but heck I needed some toothpaste and a haircut; not really giving much thought to the countless IEDs that were regularly placed by the road, and post-explosive evidence of them every mile or so, and the possibility of sniper fire.

So we had the usual briefing about the wearing of body armour and we were off for a day's shopping.

One particular day we also needed supplies for the chow hall. These would be picked up, and pretty much the only other reason worth going for as well was a blissfully cold mocha-latte-frappuccino with extra shots of espresso as it would be a week or two until the next one.

Everything was done in doubles where possible, so we had two ten-wheeled trucks called PLS (Palletised Loading System), in case one broke down. About half way there, doing about 70mph or as fast as they could be pushed, I was in the passenger seat of the number two vehicle, when there was an explosion, not an overly big one, but an explosion none the less. It hit the front vehicle and I had a ringside seat.

My first thoughts were 'that was a good shot, right next to the PLS'. My second thought was 'I hope the guys driving it were OK'. There was some smoke coming from it but it remained on the road and appeared to be in control. By this time we had driven through the smoke from the explosion, which had a really strong smell of propellant, I was expecting to see smoke then flames coming from the lead PLS. However, there was nothing, they just kept going and I couldn't imagine what emergency action was going on inside the cab. The weird thing was it was almost like watching it on the internet, it didn't feel real at all, but my heart never skipped a beat as to what could happen next or even what was happening right then. I remained quite calm, but it was real. Not being able to stop as we were now in the 'killing zone' which was usually the first kilometre after an IED hit, and if the vehicle was disabled, a small arms ambush could take place, so we pushed on until we got to our destination.

PLS

Everybody checked out OK and no-one was injured.

The passenger had previously been hit six times by roadside bombs during his time in Iraq with hardly any scratches, but he said they were wearing a bit thin now and he was looking forward to his two weeks off in Thailand. With minor damage to the PLS and a replaced tyre, stores loaded, coffee drunk, toiletries bought and the shopping lists for nuts, chocolate and cigarettes fulfilled, it was home for some roast turkey. The journey back went without any further incident … Just another day in Iraq.

PLEASE TO BE ALIVE – AGAIN!

You'd think Iraqi military and police checkpoints were a good thing but during this time in Iraq for the military and contractors, not so much. Firstly, being a choke point, if you got stuck at a checkpoint this made you vulnerable to attack from wherever, either by small arms, RPG fire or the close placement of an IED. So there were a number of actions …

'Drive it like you stole it'. This was mentioned a number of times but in the larger vehicles it was not so easy due to limited manoeuvrability. They pushed through none the less, sometimes causing damage to the vehicle and checkpoint but saving lives by opening up the checkpoint allowing easier passage for the others in the convoy to pass unhindered.

There was another way, where possible. This happened to me a few times but the first time was the most memorable and that was to bypass the checkpoint on the opposite side of the road known as 'suicide'.

The American convoy commander announced over the radio, "We're going hot, we're going suicide." My immediate thoughts were of those films where all the cars coming towards you swerve out of the way, crash into each other or with you in a head-on smash.

'Should be interesting', I thought and braced myself for the ride of my life.

It was like being in an action movie but for real. Initially I was ready for any possible impact as we crossed the medium, but the lead convoy vehicles warn all the oncoming cars of our approach and they steer clear. This works well and it wasn't long before we had bypassed the checkpoint, crossed back to our original side of the road and onwards with our journey.

For whatever reason, local holiday, bad weather, we would keep ourselves occupied by some means, first aid training, not really advanced stuff but as it says first aid, inserting saline drips, how and where to inject morphine, dragging an exposed badly injured person out of the line of fire to cover or what to do in the event of an IED strike on a convoy.

On one such occasion was a 'driver down drill'. With a few of the works vehicles and in groups of 4 or 5, we headed to a nice straight bit of road to practice. The scenario was as follows; the vehicle you are in is hit by an IED and the driver is severely injured and unable to drive. This means the front passenger takes control of the steering wheel, cocks a leg over and accelerates out of the kill zone if possible, failing that wait for a push from the vehicle from your rear. Meanwhile the rear passenger leans over, puts the back of the driver's seat down and unclips his seat belt, the driver is then pulled by the rear passenger to the rear of the vehicle and the front passenger slides into the driver's seat. This was all done on the move. What great fun we all had in practicing this but thankfully it was training none of us had to use.

-

My last day and demobilisation, I was going home. For the last time we had to face the hour-long drive to the Tikrit base. I had survived nine months in one of the most dangerous places in the world and had just one last hour to get through before I was truly safe from the carnage.

We were told to look out for snipers on the roof tops, and debris on the road which could be hiding that fatal IED.

I looked furtively at every roof top and every brick, rubbish bag and anything that looked in the remotest bit suspicious - nothing. I think that this last trip out was such an adrenaline hit that when we finally arrived at the base, within 20 minutes I was fighting to stay awake and was totally drained, mentally and physically. I HAD MADE IT!

We all had a few days back at El Paso before we were completely done. We handed our previously issued equipment back, had a medical to see that you were as healthy as when you left and a psychologist brief to explain that the things that you had seen, done and experienced would probably have quite an impact on close relationships back home.

They said it would take around 18 months for marital relationships to settle back down. On my return to the UK my wife decided, after 6 years of marriage, that we should get divorced. Much to my shock all of my belongings had already been moved to storage at a mutual friends.

A quick divorce was granted as she had duped me into signing a separation agreement some years earlier for a different purpose, so she told me. I guess she wasn't prepared to wait 18 months. At least by now, I was out of debt.

DING DING - ROUND TWO

After a number of months away from Iraq, word on the grapevine was that there was a new contract going called the 'Coalition Munitions Clearance Project'. This was to remove and destroy any previously available explosives from Saddam's vast stockpile that the insurgents had access to and to reduce the number of IEDs being made, as it was a major problem because so many were dying on a daily basis.

This time it was to be with a different company.

I was now divorced, free and single. Having had such a good time previously, again I jumped at the chance. Same people, different job. This time I would be doing UXO clearance.

Due to the economics of the whole contracting business, costs were cut across the board.

So this meant not going to the US for another holiday - oh well.

Nonetheless, I had a ten-minute interview over the phone, some paper work to fill in and another medical at my old haunt, Harley Street. I was given a clean bill of health and off I went again.

A ten-minute interview? At the last count there were only about 8,000 bomb disposalers worldwide and as such they make up quite a small professional body and form a fairly closed shop. So generally, the conversations about references went like this…

"Does anyone know 'such and such'?"

"Yeah he's a dick." That's as far as it goes. So far I have managed to avoid that … I think.

Apparently, and you might have heard this elsewhere, there are only six degrees of separation in the world (on average) from someone you know, who knows someone, who knows someone … who knows you.

In EOD that is probably reduced to two. There is one Scottish bomb disposaler called Angus who is probably known to all 7999! On every job I have been on there is generally someone who knows someone you know or Angus.

It's a great family and you always have a comrade in arms.

After all, your life might depend on them one day and vice versa.

It was September 7th 2007 and still hot at 115°F plus. Baghdad and Camp Victory were a familiar sight this time and a lot less daunting than the first. I even knew where the chow hall was and felt so much more relaxed. The company compound was at the same place as before the companies had swapped out.

After meeting the project manager and finding out what I was to be doing and where I was going, this time to Michigan, I was just so elated and looking forward to going to work.

There was a lot of waiting time between places, sometimes days being in Iraq.

It once took Neil Sprankle (to whom this book is dedicated) 28 days to get back to the work site following his arrival. He was told to get a helicopter to one base, then go on to another base, sometimes going to the same base twice for a more advantageous route onwards, and so on, with a few days waiting in between each. By the time he finally arrived back at work, he had done almost a complete tour of every base in Iraq and reduced his work time by a quarter.

On leaving Baghdad we passed the infamous Abu Ghraib prison, known for its less than humane treatment of its prisoners in the early days by the American Army Reserve. Nowadays it is known as Baghdad Central Prison.

We continued West passing Ramadi on the left, at about the half way point - this was the most dangerous place in the world, for sure.

We arrived at Michigan aka Lake Michigan (which in total is about 2 ½ hours driving from Baghdad), the lake is nothing more than a scrape in the ground with some dubious murky water in the bottom about 700 metres from the accommodation/living area, but I think it was used for our portable water which probably saved a lot of money.

This time I was to be living in a converted lorry container. On their own they're quite big but these are partitioned off into 3 rooms and accommodating 2 people per room. I only had a bed and a wardrobe with about a 2-foot width of floor space the length of the bed between the two. The wardrobes were in the centre of the room and acted like a partition between the 2 bed spaces and afforded a bit of privacy.

The containers weren't the safest places to live and ours caught fire due to the dodgy electrics. This was quite a regular occurrence on the many sites around Iraq and almost gutted the room next door. This caused some smoke damage in our room but after some cleaning and some air freshener it was almost as good as new again.

I spent almost 9 months living in this tiny space, with a few pictures of my daughter on the wall, and a real good friend called Andy, who I had worked with before Iraq (and still do) as a roommate.

I realised that I really didn't need or want much more than this and was quite content with life.

In ordnance, we work on generics, then things go a bit deeper from then on.

How it all works is basically was it dropped, thrown, propelled or laid? How? If it was propelled for example, how was it propelled; by gun, rocket or catapult? What shape is it; straight sided, round, does it have any pointy bits on it? What colour and markings? What is its country of origin? Where and when was it used, WWI, WWII or present day etc?

So there are an awful lot of bombs and bullets from all over the world still out there waiting to be recovered and destroyed, and so much of it was in Iraq in all the above categories, and so many more.

-

On my first day at work, I was clearing a blown-up ammunition bunker. This consisted of a few LNs (as few as we could use as we got the job done almost as quick without them), a few UXO techs, team leader etc. We also used a 360° armoured digger to scrape through wreckage to expose the UXO. It was then removed by hand, collected up and put in the AHA (Ammunition Holding Area) at the end of the day ready for demolition.

AHA

There had been some major damage to the bunker itself, possibly caused by an explosion. Saddam's storage protocol of 'compatible explosive stores' included not storing the dangerous stuff (explosives) with the really dangerous stuff (detonators) as one can set the other off if there is an accident, so they are kept in separate buildings.

In the Iraqi arsenal there were ... none.

You never know what you were going to find or in what state it would be, so safety precautions for us were of prime importance.

It was still hot throughout the day at around 115°F but slowly cooling down. Luckily, I had missed the hottest part of the year and the weekly rota was the same as on the last project. (Oh yeah, the thing that my dear old geography teacher told me about the desert, hot in the day, freezing at night? Rubbish, it's bloody hot at night too!)

We were wearing 45lbs of full upper body armour with attached carabiner clips to hang water and electrical tape (some essential tools of the trade) and blood group Velcro patches.

My blood group B negative isn't the rarest but I have read that less than 2% of the population have it so it's always good to find out if anyone else on your site is the same. I was lucky on this site it was almost 10%, lucky for all of us really and as a fellow B neg once told me, "It's not just a blood group, it's a way of life."

I donned a Kevlar helmet with safety goggles to keep the dust out, and big thick gloves, and set about humping and dumping 100mm of armour piercing bullet heads weighing around 35lbs each and 120mm mortars weighing in at around 25lbs, for most of the day.

The first few days I struggled with the heat, the body armour and the physical work, as I hadn't lifted much over 20lbs for quite a few years. By about day three of being back in the saddle and after a chilli con carne ration pack meal called an MRE (Meal Ready to Eat) for lunch, it was more than I could cope with and was violently sick, much to the amusement of all around. I remember thinking to myself, 'this is your life now, so get on with it'. I was soon in the full swing of things and from there on it was up and up.

Finally, after a few weeks my first bunker was finished, metal free and so on to the next one.

This one was totally different from the last one in the way it had sort of collapsed in on itself with blowtorch cut holes in the metal structure and not so damaged. It had been started some months earlier and paused due to some of the initial stuff that had been found, some quite sensitive 3.5" rockets, aka bazooka rockets.

With these, when the spring loaded safety pin is removed or had popped out, it had a sliding inertia weight inside which can very easily set the rocket warhead off, so it was vital to be very, very careful with them as we came across them.

We removed most of the surface stuff which included 160mm mortars and were given the nickname tuna fish, as well as the obligatory 100mm bloody heavy ones, before we brought in the 360° digger again. We started sinking our teeth into the bunker and within a few weeks we had broken the back of it and had about six or seven metres left, when something caught my eye. 'It looked like a bone', I thought.

Then one or two more showed up, so I called my colleague over for some sort of confirmation on what I was seeing, but he wasn't all that versed in anatomy, or EOD for that matter. The same bloke almost caused a major accident due to complacency later on in his tour, which could have taken out two others with himself. This was swept well under the carpet and no one got injured. Complacency is never a good thing in our job!

After looking around a bit more I found a human mandible, some more scrapings and a few more bits of skull ... Time to call the management in.

When they arrived in force, one of them said, "Nope, animal bones."

I pointed out to him that I was an ex-dental technician and I knew people's teeth when I saw them.

On telling the rest of the management, I was then told that I was unable to confirm that they were indeed human remains as I was not a medic, oh well...

As we cleared further and further into the bunker, the smell was quite bad and changed in intensity at different times but in an odd sort of way, it is a smell I have always wanted to experience. We cleared out bones and bits of mummified bodies for a few days, all the time I was trying to compare the smell to something I knew. My final conclusion was that the smell was a cross between Marmite and Bovril! It was all I could smell, on my clothes and up my nose.

To prevent us from being accused of desecration of the bones we used LNs to pick them up, they put them either into black bags or empty MRE boxes before being given to the local Mullah for ID and burial.

MACABRE REMAINS

None of the internationals were bothered by this due to the relationship between the insurgents and the coalition, they considered it more of an inconvenience and a hindrance to getting the bunker cleared. Knowing a little bit about anatomy I knew that there is only one sacrum per person and while I was there I counted about seven unless I missed any, and looking at the teeth, they were aged from about 17 to mid- 30s.

While this bunker was being cleared along with others in the same manner, a recently arrived Supervisor called Frank from Alaska thought that clearance in this way was laboriously slow and time consuming, and after a lot of calculations, that it would take years to clear them all using this method.

He shared an idea that could speed things up somewhat. This entailed pulling down the metal structure using a 360, to move the metal roofing clear of the remaining debris, then using a large seven tonne bulldozer to push the remaining mixture of dirt and ammo out over a large area, spreading it over hundreds of metres, whilst a UXO tech walked only a short distance from the 'dozer blade and on seeing any UXO, stop the 'dozer to retrieve it.

'WHAT?! Won't the ordnance be detonating all the time'?

I think that we all thought the same thing; 'well that's our life expectancy shortened'.

To begin with, all of us were quite sceptical of this method and didn't want to adopt it so we remained a long distance away from the 'dozer blade whilst watching for ordnance to pop up and come to the surface. But as time went by and confidence grew, this became the standard method of operations.

EARLY MORNING DOZING

This debris was spread out over such a large area and was done one thin slice at a time, so that nothing was missed. Then the bunker had to be levelled down to ground level and blended into the surrounding ground.

One thing it did mean was that during the day we had to walk several miles and drink even more water (sometimes up to 2 gallons a day). Instead of taking sometimes a month or more, this operation was cut down to a few days per bunker. I think it cut the project by over 18 months and nobody was ever injured using this method. Another job 'jobbed'.

As I mentioned earlier, no large pieces of ordnance ever detonated or functioned as they should have done but that's not to say nothing ever went bang.

As and when things *do* go bang I try not to allow my startle reflex to kick in and try to maintain an outward appearance of calm. If any flying bits are going to hit you they will. When clearing one of the bunkers and using the old method of clearing, the digger driver was scraping the ground and it was my stint on watch.

I was on top of the outside of the bunker peering in with just my head exposed to the line of fire, should anything go off.

It did but I never twitched - I was quite pleased with myself. The bucket of the digger had come down on a 40mm anti-aircraft shell setting the cartridge off.

I waited for the driver to carry on, but nothing. After about 30 seconds he jumped out of his cab and started running away in the opposite direction as fast as he could, making some sort of screeching noise. He wasn't injured in any way, I started laughing, wondering why he was running away when the drama was already over.

When I eventually caught up with him, he thought that more would explode. I explained to him that one was done and that if anything else was to go it would have already happened.

It was just funny that he had waited so long before deciding to make his escape.

A week or so after the bunker was done and another started, it was demolition day. Now this was a really special thing for me and what I had been hankering after during my whole time spent in Iraq.

It had been almost 20 years since my last hands-on demolition.

The excitement was just unbearable for me and I felt like a kid at Christmas. I was just so happy, it's what I have wanted to do all my life. So as you can imagine, I was quite looking forward to it.

We had our fifth or sixth briefing of the day and it was still early o'clock, the explosives had been issued and off we went to the range to set up the shots.

DEMO PREP

Everyone was in great spirits which was the usual atmosphere on the range. The demo pits had been cleared earlier in the week and we had a nice flat platform to work on. The UXO was laid out, some already in boxes, known as shot boxes, small stuff on the bottom, fuses and the like then the progressively larger stuff on top in order to blow up the smaller stuff, so that it went into the ground and not up and thrown everywhere, which would cause a problem later on. Then this was followed by a smoke break, a quick ten minutes.

The C4 explosives were dished out, and what a lot there was! It was put into the numerous pits which were about four or five metres wide and over a metre deep. The explosives were put in, laid over everything, primer blocks made and detonating cord attached which was used to connect everything together, and the whole lot topped off like any great cake with the candles and all the illumination mortars. This makes the shot look great with sparkling lights.

Everything is now covered with the surrounding dirt to help contain the effects of shrapnel and fragmentation. All that remained was to connect the detonators.

Two people stayed behind for this job while the rest retreated to the firing point. Detonators were connected and the final two people were back at the firing point. All security checks made, and all's clear.

Any aircraft overhead? Air-Movements had been notified some days before and they had a tendency to fly nearby to watch too. A glance skyward; no aircraft, one more quick look … "Fire in the hole, fire in the hole, fire in the hole!"

I counted, one, two. The first sign that the shot had gone was all 2000lbs of net explosives creating a massive and rapidly expanding cloud of dust and sparkling lights, a few seconds later, the 'BANG!' Great, first shot successfully over.

"Shot out, 1205," was the radio announcement.

I felt a great sense of pride and satisfaction at this point, as I had endured hardship and austere conditions, risked life and limb on several occasions and knowing that I might have prevented loss of lives, a very real feeling of a positive achievement.

DEMO SHOT

During my initial few months at Michigan, I needed a Christmas card picture and had already decided on the theme; a big bang in the background, a 'Merry Christmas' placard, and me.

MERRY CHRISTMAS FROM HARRY!

On one of the shots Neil and myself were at the explosive storage area, this was a few hundred metres away from the firing point but closer to the shot with no obstructions.

Prior to the shot we did a few test firings with my camera of ourselves, and as the shot went off with me holding my placard, several shots were taken in quick succession. It was perfect and the exact result I wanted!

A few days before Christmas, the 21st I think, one of our convoys got hit and three of our security team were killed and one seriously injured. It was times like these that made me ponder on my own situation.

Hearing stories from work colleges about the UXO tech, under pressure to get the job done, was carrying more than a few suspect fuses, he dropped one which detonated, killing him. It's a risk we are all aware of and which could happen at any time.

Every morning without fail, I woke up thinking that I might not see morning tea break today, or that today would be the day and if it was I hoped it would be instantaneous and total. I would like to think I could live with the loss of a limb, possibly even two, as so many people are, but if I was comatose with tubes hanging out of me, that was a different matter. Or on the other hand, if through my own stupidity I killed or maimed someone else, I don't think I could live with myself. Yet if I were to be killed by someone else's stupidity then I know in my soul or whatever there is, I would forgive them.

On Christmas Day 2007 at Michigan, so as not to let us ponder on recent sad events, family and home, the management wanted to keep us and our minds busy, so it was decided a few days earlier to get all the notifications in place, and we would do a demolition.

This was mainly going to be a white phosphorous (aka WP or Wiley Pete or Willy P) shot. There are some major differences between this and a normal explosive shot in the manner in which it is always either blown up into the air or squashed together, and this caused some debate on the day.

It is never blown into the ground as the WP just gets spread everywhere, smokes a lot and contaminates the soil as it's active on exposure to air.

At breakfast there were lots of Santa hats on, the standard bunch of briefings made, then off to the range. It was a cold and crisp morning and as usual not a cloud in the sky, the sun was soon up and we were all a bit warmer.

Again, spirits were good and the shot carried out in the usual manner with great visual effect.

Hooray, half day, everything was packed up and we all went back to camp, washed up for a right hearty and stunning Christmas Day meal. To this day it was one of my most memorable Christmases - it's not every Christmas that you get to blow stuff up!

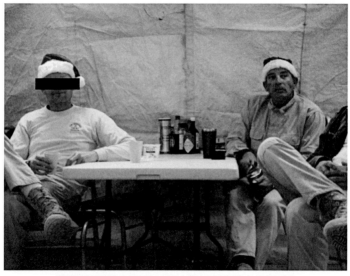

CHRISTMAS BREAKFAST BRIEF & DEMO

MERRY CHRISTMAS!

A few days later on our day off, I rose quite early, and opened the door…

"Wow, guess what?" I said to Andy. "There's about an inch and a half of snow on the ground."

"Bollocks!" was the swift reply.

It was the first time it had snowed for a long time and in Baghdad the first time in over 80 years. So everyone was up and out in the snow, throwing snowballs and taking pictures. We had a great international logistical support team. It consisted of Indians and Filipinos. Some of the Filipinos had never seen snow in their entire lives, so not much work was done by them in the early morning. By mid-day there was not a trace that the snow had ever been there. A nice respite.

DESERT SNOW

Not long after this, Neil almost cost me a day of lost wage indirectly. It was always being drummed into us that if we were late for our 6am meeting which started on the dot, then we would not be going to work that day and lose a day's pay but as the week went on we started to accrue overtime which was worth having.

I don't think anyone was ever late with that carrot dangling.

I had just arrived back off leave, what with the difference in time from the UK and the rigmarole of getting back to site and being up at all times of the day and night, my body clock didn't know if it was coming or going.

My first night back, I stayed awake all night and couldn't sleep a wink, before the second night had arrived, Neil said he had some sleeping tablets, "OK I'll take one." A small white pill was produced from his room, no instructions on when to take it as it was my first ever. Again that night, I tried in vain to sleep without the little white pill, I eventually took it at around midnight, again, nothing and was in the wide awake club again all night.

On night three, Neil said he had a different sort, a big blue gelatine liquid filled capsule, again given with no instruction. My understanding of sleeping pills was that they knocked you out for 4 hours or so, wore off then the last 4 or so hours was natural sleep, not the case apparently.

Midnight, I was still awake, 'OK I'll take the blue pill'. I think within 5 minutes I was out like a light.

At 05:55am I heard, "Harry! Harry, wake up! You'll be late for the meeting!"

As fast as I could, I was dressed and in the meeting by 6am, I don't know how but I had made it and I was still ¾ asleep. Turns out that these horse tranquillisers last for a whole 8 hours and sure enough by about 08:30am I was now fully awake and fit for work once again.

-

A few months went by and whilst clearing more bunkers we found some good stuff; 120mm rockets, fuses, the usual 100mm lumps, RPGs, more white phosphorus, tunas and more.

One of the bunkers had a round hole in the roof and a round hole in the floor. A big bomb had hit but not exploded as the bunker was still intact, so it needed to be retrieved.

I think at the time it was unknown whether it was a British 1000 pounder as we had found evidence of Tornado-dropped stuff elsewhere on the site, or an American Mk84 2000 pounder.

The Brits were deployed, which was great for our morale, including two ex-squaddies Jim and Paddy, and ex-crab, Andy. (This name 'crab', or 'crab-fat' to give it its full title came about like this: RAF people are regularly known by this name in the other two services, I was told many, many years ago that when Matelots caught crabs (the lice not the crustacean!), the protective grease that was on Naval shells, which was a sort of blue gunk, was found to be the perfect remedy, and since this matched the colour of the old RAF uniform, the name stuck. Anyway, I digress!

There were a total of three crabs Andy, Chris and myself on this project, so this would have been a great coup for the camaraderie amongst us three if Andy had found it. But after quite a bit of searching, nothing was found, and his opposite number Paddy, an ex-Royal Engineer, decided to have a play with the detector near the hole and he did find it. It was quite some time before Andy lived that down.

2000 POUNDER FOUND EVENTUALLY

As the days started getting longer and hotter again, we left the camp, stopped off at the detector pit to do our daily check of our metal detectors before heading off to our respective work sites. Several trucks headed off in convoy down the main drag of the site, one by one we peeled off left and right.

The sun was rising with an amazing red glow and I was thinking to myself, 'this is brilliant, no M25, no traffic jams, no speed cameras, no bus lane cameras, no yellow box junction cameras, no cameras watching every move I make and no queues. Free food, free internet, free accommodation, dealing with Saddam's leftovers, finding weird and wonderful stuff and blowing it up, great wildlife, working with great like-minded blokes, great weather and we hadn't seen any rain for months'.

This was history in the making, and we were getting paid for it. I got quite emotional and I didn't think life could get much better, but I was wrong.

By March, I ended up coming off bunkers and working with Jim and Paddy, both great blokes on the demo team, an absolute dream come true. This was a really good thing on so many levels. Firstly, you are pretty much left to your own devices and left to get on with the job in hand.

Secondly, working with Brits is somewhat different to working in a multinational team, as we had all served in the British military and all had received exactly the same training.

Thirdly, we all understood each other and nothing was lost in translation and together our work ethic was seamless. Apart, that is, from preparing the demo range for the next shot and getting the ordnance to the range and making preparations for an ammunition burn.

An ammunition burn consists of small arms ammunition and other non-exploding ordnance, flares, smoke pots and smoke grenades, even captured rifle magazines being burnt rather than blown up because it's cheaper.

You have a big hole, fill it full of wood, put the ammunition on top, cover in fuel, light blue touch paper and leave it for a day and the result is (if it all goes well), all the ammunition is cooked off and you should be left with empty cases and bullet heads. There are the odd kick-outs but when you are burning tens of thousands of pounds it can be expected.

Obviously there is a lot more refinement to the process, but that is the basis of it and it's great to watch and hear.

BURN PIT

AFTERMATH

We also had code 'H' to deal with. Every fortnight or so, a bunch of lorries would turn up and off-load their containers and take the empties away. 'Hmmm, what was in the containers'?

It was always like Christmas and I was always excited as to what we would discover.

In some it was all the same, maybe a bunch of 155mm artillery shells or 90mm high explosive projectiles, in another a whole load of American hand grenades that had been issued to the military and were either damaged or expired. There were 40mm rifle grenades looking like a salt or pepper pot with a golden tip, affectionately known as 'golden eggs', boxes and boxes of different types of helicopter or aircraft ammunition, maybe some small arms ammunition from everywhere either captured or just no good.

There was always at least one container that had a bunch of small interesting stuff in it such as different types of sabotage firing devices and the odd looking piece of equipment which disappeared quite easily surrounded by loads of C4 explosives as did all the ordnance we had sorted through and that the other teams had recovered from the site.

In fact, on one occasion, Andy had been working there and told me at the end of the day that while they were sorting out the small arms they had found a bunch of ammunition with swastikas and eagles on them, and these included the clips.

'The clips would make a great souvenir!' I thought. I had heard the first time I was in Iraq they had been seen elsewhere and I wanted to see for myself. I had been looking out for them since my first time there, but never did get to see any. I asked him what he had done with them and he said they were in the shot boxes that were three quarters filled with ammunition, so they had thousands and thousands of bullets in each (there were eight or nine shot boxes).

'So close, yet so far,' I thought. In the morning, Paddy and myself started looking furtively for them, it took us ten minutes and I think we found them all and their clips, who would have thought it.

FROM ONE DICTATOR TO ANOTHER

By now I was quite skilful in the art of forklifting and it was one of my main jobs on the demo team. I loved it, moving the dodgier ammunition in the shot boxes from the AHA to the demo range probably about a mile away at a few miles per hour over bumps and holes. It was quite therapeutic as there was never any real urgency and it was not something you'd want to rush anyway. It got moved as and when and gave me loads of time to ponder life and generally daydream, soaking up the sun and enjoying the scenery, wildlife and the massive blue sky. I'd also fork all the ammunition off the PLS to where it was needed; this took up the majority of most days between sorting Code H, stacking and demolition days.

I was having such an amazing time seeing and doing stuff the 'Joe-public' doesn't generally see. Some weeks earlier I had bought myself a *Sanyo Xacti*, a small and fairly cheap palm sized video camera on a day out to the military base at Ramadi, on one of the fortnightly toothpaste runs. I thought I could document what I did for a living to show to friends at home and it would be a bit of a keepsake for the blokes I worked with.

So over the next two weeks I recorded everything that moved and if it didn't I kicked it until it moved and then videoed it. I interviewed almost everyone with the same three questions:

"Who are you, where are you from and what are you doing here?"

Some of the answers were quite varied from, 'on the run from the CSA (Child Support Agency)', to 'it wasn't me, I didn't do it'. This was done at various times and places throughout the day.

I also wanted to include some close-up shots of the demolitions by just leaving the camera running close to the shot. I achieved a fair amount of success and after some late nights/early mornings and with the task of editing, my film was over.

The camera lasted well in the heat and dust but almost succumbed on another site when it was placed about 70 metres from a 100-ton shot. The camera did survive but the view screen was shattered. Even after this episode, it was still usable but needed a visual sighting on the shots and lasted right up to the end of my contract.

-

I mentioned that it was always hot, but occasionally we would get sandstorms, some were localised and some had been travelling for days. Just before they hit there would be a massive wall of sand and dust heading our way.

These would sometimes last for a few days, the finest dust almost like talcum powder would cover and get into all sorts of things, from engine filters to computers and shortened its life somewhat.

It also made breathing difficult and was almost impossible to smoke. Goggles were an absolute essential; without them, vision was impossible. One of the best personal protections was the shemagh as it kept the fine dust out of your lungs.

There were two parts to this site, the bit that we had been working on and another, a not very talked about area where no one was allowed to go.

When mentioned it was called the Chemical Area.

A FAST APPROACHING SANDSTORM

It covered quite a large area and originally had some large storage warehouses, but they had all be raised to the ground and only debris and the hard standings remained.

As the bunkers were almost finished the majority of the teams were moved to the Chemical Area and after a week or so it was renamed the Purple Area. Some clearance did happen but it was deemed to be just too dodgy and I think that people who were getting paid a lot less than us (the military) ended up with the job.

I did have a few outings to the area, this was to clear some of the unexploded sub-munitions as they littered the place, by BIP'ing them (blow in place) and to generally snout around the area.

THE PURPLE AREA

We found some interesting stuff, loads of large weapon packaging, the odd gas mask, modified rockets and a fair few partially buried and exposed large

Russian and Spanish looking air dropped bombs with painted hazard rings around them which denoted 'chemical'.

But with all the exposure to the sand and sun no proper ID was made or ever discussed as to what they might have contained. I don't know what ever happened to them actually, a few days later after first seeing them, I went on leave. I never saw Neil again.

-

We were given a few weeks off, a visit to Walt Disney World Resort in Florida with my daughter then back to Baghdad. The flight back in was from Kuwait by Hercules and the plane was loaded with hairy-arsed American Marines. It was night-time and the physical feeling we all received on that flight was ten times better than any of the rides I had just been on at Disney World.

Maybe that could be suggested to Disney? It seemed as if we were at a great height over Baghdad in order to avoid any missile, rocket or small arms attacks, but we had arrived in a safe column of airspace.

Then in a seemingly endless downward spiralling motion we dropped in large increments and every few minutes we plummeted several hundred feet with loads of negative G causing our internals to almost become our externals. It felt as if we were encountering major turbulence, but we were not, it was all part of the plan.

I love extreme flying and had the honour of an hour's flight in a Tornado when I was in the RAF, many years earlier. It was quite an experience, watching a bunch of steely eyed killers with looks of fear on their faces, who eventually one by one reached for the sick bags. Probably not what the plane actually did, but that is what it seemed like. That was one of the best flights I have ever had, if only Ryanair did flights like that!

-

With my feet back on terra-firma, a new location beckoned, this time a place called Normandy. To this day, I have absolutely no idea geographically where it is or what its real name is.

On arrival there were a bunch of familiar faces along with new ones with no names, and a bunch of names that I could now put faces to. Again, I was going to be on the demo team, great, that instantly put me in a good frame of mind.

I was initially put in a tent, quite a big tent but there were only two of us in there.

After a few hours chatting, there was an almighty bang and the air overpressure almost collapsed the tent inwards and my face must have looked a picture.

I was swiftly informed that there was a 155mm gun on the base, but where? Again, I don't know. We went outside and after about 45 seconds we saw a flare light up in the distance, I was told it was towards Iran. There were normally a few of these nightly occasions and they never failed to make me jump.

The following day I was given a base tour. It was an old British military base from back in the 20s and the architecture was typical of the military bases in Cyprus; square, long and white with pillars holding the veranda up.

There was even a cenotaph, except this one had a damaged picture of Saddam on it. The place still had the old guard towers which all looked like they had been there for decades.

Just outside our T-walled compound was an interrogation block. I had heard that sometimes in the middle of the night there were sinister comings and goings, but I never saw or heard anything more than that.

A CASTELLATED BUNKER

One of the requisites of being at Normandy was that you had to reach a basic shooting competency set by the US Army with a rifle and pistol.

We had a morning on the 25-metre shooting range, this was the first time I had fired a high-powered rifle that was properly sighted-in and after a few practice magazines the test began. Parts of the targets simulated 300 metres range.

On completion of this we had the pistol test, stand, squat and walking towards the target while firing.

At the end of this I was three points off marksman and achieved sharpshooter grade.

Although some people might disagree with this, to be revealed later.

The demo range had a blown-up tank on it, this was used by special forces for demo techniques so there were quite a few big bits spread out all over the place with a lot of holes punched through here and there at strategic points.

To the back of the demo hole there was a bit of a hill. I was to be working with two very experienced techs; Steve a Brit and John from across the pond and they both taught me a lot. We even had some playtime during a shot when we made a huge Union Jack flag on the hill with detonating cord, and with my camera running, the shot fired as usual. When we returned to check the shot and collect my camera we found that there wasn't enough time to record it, so we never got to see an exploding Union Jack.

On one part of the camp there was a huge graveyard of captured enemy vehicles and anti-aircraft guns, we managed to gain entry and spent the next few hours posing and taking more pictures than you can shake a stick at and we even tried removing any nice shiny loose bits for souvenirs.

Normandy was a nice change and again I met some great people, but I was only there for about six weeks before the task was complete.

THE GUN GRAVEYARD

Next stop, Bayji Ammunition Depot, next to one of the largest oil refinery towns in Northern Iraq, if not the whole country. It was formerly known as Arlington - yep, I was on my way back to my first ever workplace in Iraq.

This time was going to be completely different though; as we lived on site, so there was no daily gauntlet to run, which was a relief. The job this time was all the ammunition I had previously been involved in sorting was to be destroyed.

I arrived again to see a whole bunch of familiar faces, so I felt right at home.

The demolition range was some four or five miles away right at the other end of the site and had two usable massive scrapes in the ground with traverses either side and from end to end, maybe 500 metres in length.

The rotation was a shot every second or third day, there would be three shots of around 100 tonnes, each being detonated almost simultaneously. We couldn't wait to see the first one of this size, but first of all we had to set up our shot.

There were about six of us on a team and when we needed them, we brought the LNs in to help with the humping and dumping of 100mm after 100mm weighing around 48 lbs each of all different flavours averaging about 3000 of them per team, 9000 in total.

Again, they were mostly Russian in origin and as a surface protection they were covered in a weird coating called cosmoline and generally covered everyone. Line after line of whole cartridges were laid out side by side, sometimes three high.

Next was to place the C4; this was only done by the internationals and the LNs were removed for other tasks. One or two pallets of explosives arrived, and the boxes broken out and spread along the lines.

Then the C4 could be placed on top, line after line of it, each block touching the next in order to achieve continuity of the explosive shock wave. The charge blocks were added and the whole lot connected by reels and reels of detonating cord.

A break was now in order to drink more water and eat an MRE for late breakfast. These had been placed in the back of the truck first thing in the morning, so by now they were so hot that they had to be blown on to cool them down before you could eat them. I have had to comment in restaurants on several occasions that, 'I have eaten hotter food warmed by the sun than you are serving here'. Restaurant owners, take note.

PART OF A 100 TONNE SHOT

We then cleaned all the trash up and placed it on the shot. Almost all connected, camera in position, just needed to roll the camera, connect up the detonators, then we were ready to blow.

This was the largest shot I was about to witness by far, everyone was now back at the firing point and the usual security checks.

"Clear to the North?"

"Clear," followed by checks to the remaining cardinal points, to confirm there was no one in the danger zone. Occasionally, locals including mothers carrying babies, tried to get as close to the shot as they could in order to collect any pieces of brass casing flying their way. They would hide in holes in the ground so as not to be hit by flying fragmentation and would try to sell the scrap for a few dollars. So a secure vigil was always kept to ensure no one entered.

READY TO GO AND BLOW

Warning given … "Fire in the hole, fire in the hole, fire in the hole, counting, one, two."

Then almost instantaneously three massive balls of bright orange fire ascended turning into massive darkening mushroom clouds. We were all stood on top of one of the bunkers to get an advantageous view, then several seconds later, 'BANG' and at the same time the shock wave hit us which pressed my trousers to my legs for an instant.

Having watched the shot go off, in all the excitement of trying to take in and process what I had just seen, I had completely forgotten about the sound and almost crapped myself.

3X 100 TONNE SHOT

Several shots later, a consignment of captured weapons had arrived and needed to be destroyed. We didn't know what was in the container and wanted to be amongst the first there, just to be nosy and to pilfer any available souvenirs like telescopic sights or bayonets.

A bunch of us went to peruse the wares, I was with Chris, a crab mate of mine from our previous site, who was an avid gun collector, so much so he moved to the US to pursue his obsession. Within seconds he had a WWII German assault rifle, an ultra rare StG 44 in his hands. I was given its full history, a few seconds more I was given its serial number 4022, everything matched. I was told that there was only ever about 20,000 made and in its current slightly rusted condition it was still worth around $50,000. He was distraught as within a few hours it would be destroyed with explosives among many other WWI & WWII guns and various models of the AK47 and two old British military 9mm sub machine guns.

The last shot we did here before shipping out was an explosive demolition it consisted of surplus explosives C4 and some old stock TNT blocks, too dangerous to move anywhere as this would have been a most valuable cargo to the insurgents.

PLEASE, PLEASE, PLEASE!

AFTER 8.5 TONNES OF EXPLOSIVES

We travelled back to Baghdad to find out whether we still had a job or would be sent home. My ID card had now expired and I knew I would have problems getting onto the base because of the stringent security.

Our vehicle commander suggested to the client rep from the US Corps of Engineers that he could use his ID to get me onto the base. First there was a look of amazement then a thought process and then the reply, "Did you really just ask a government representative that?"

The vehicle commander, being a Brit, had a quick reply and said something like, "Just checking!"

As we arrived at the weapon unloading area, secure but not quite at the checkpoint, he told me to get out and swap vehicles as we needed to use another entrance to get me in. It was a big fat armoured one, like the vehicle in the film, *Dumb and Dumber*.

In the back was a load of luggage, I was told to hide under it, which I did with only my eyes poking out. If I had been found it would have meant the rubber glove treatment for all of us, for sure. That was how I ended up back at our compound for the good or bad news.

Is the suspense killing you? It was me. I so wanted to stay, as did all of us. Despite the dangers it was an awesome way of life and so varied day in day out, both emotionally and physically.

As it happened, I was allowed to stay. I was ecstatic.

This time I was going to Forward Operating Base Hammer, with the MC Hammer song, *'You Can't Touch This'* always being sung; well the *'Hammer Time'* bit anyway. Once again, I had no idea where it was that I was going, I didn't really care either.

So, a few days more in Baghdad, then *'Hammer Time'*, again taken by armed convoy, this time I was sat next to a SAW, (Squad Automatic Weapon). Originally, I thought it was called a 'saw' as that is what it did to people when you pulled the trigger. I was given a quick brief on how to use it if need be, then we were off.

We left the base through an exit I hadn't seen before and within ten minutes we were in downtown Baghdad. The whole place looked like a YouTube video scene, the only thing that was missing was the bomb blast, RPG or small arms fire. I had my hand on the grip and finger off the trigger. My senses heightened and everything was just so real.

Onwards we travelled with the odd horn blast from our convoy to get Iraqi cars and trucks to move out of the way.

From when I first arrived, the convoy vehicles had signs on their rear saying, DANGER, STAY BACK 100 METRES OR YOU WILL BE SHOT in English and Arabic.

This was then changed as shown below but deadly force was authorised and had been used on many occasions in case of suicide car bombers.

WARNING

As time moved on, to not be seen as too aggressive, warning flags had to be waved, water bottles thrown and verbal warnings shouted. There was talk of paintball guns being used, but the threat still remained somewhat reduced, although it was still there.

It only takes one!

We came upon a checkpoint near an overpass with quite a queue and the suicide technique was no longer allowed either but was used anyway. This seemed a perfectly normal thing to do now but due to our position, downtown Baghdad, we scooted around the checkpoint on the opposite side of the road, back to the right side of the road and onwards.

I was thinking to myself, 'if anything happens, I am there with the SAW ... Come on, let's dance' I was flooded with adrenaline.

About an hour later my adrenaline, the people, the buildings and traffic slowly disappeared and I had a huge mental crash and when I awoke, we were at the checkpoint to the entrance of FOB Hammer.

Our compound was brand new as were our rooms which even had fridges in them, a luxury. We unpacked, then in force we searched out the 'Hajji' (a term of respect for someone who had completed the Hajj pilgrimage to Mecca) DVD and electronics shop, someone needed a memory stick. We had lunch then the rest of the day off.

I was to be there for the next ten or twelve weeks when a new round of contracts was to be issued. The job was code 'H' - 'Ah, great, another load of interesting stuff to blow up'.

The demolition range was only licensed for 2000lbs so no more than that at any one time. It was quite a long way from the camp but outside a secure area down the longest straight road, again with me at the helm of the fork lift, our security always went ahead to check the area out for us.

I was told that Saddam was planning on building a big town there, but there were only the roads, drainage, pavements and loads of plots ready to be built on. There was also a whole load of dummies on sticks, probably for Iraq army training prior to the coalition arriving there.

Over the coming weeks we saw and destroyed millions of small arms ammunition from 22 caliber to massive elephant killers. We destroyed training land mines by the hundreds, American 120mm shotgun shells and even a bunch of French aircraft practice bombs and countless other things, and on the very last shot, my bicycle that I had had since Michigan was placed on the shot. We did find some bits of it but not many.

As we played back the video, you could hear bicycle bits falling to the ground. We all had a great time here, everyone got on well with each other and the work went like clockwork.

ROADSIDE IED

When we arrived back in Baghdad before de-mobbing, I'll tell you about another Brit I worked with, called Tony. He had a dubious souvenir and was thinking of ways to get it home. It was an Iraqi grenade, no explosives just the internal fragmentation sleeve and the plastic case. He decided to chance his luck and mail it home. Previously many people tried to get positively prohibited things home like live grenades and weapons, so measures were put into place to stop it. Full searches and X-rays of all parcels were carried out.

He went outside for a ciggie while they searched his box, upon his return one of the posties said, "What's this?" holding up an egg-shaped spring.

Quick on his feet he said, "Well I work for a water company back in the UK and it's part of one of the valves we use and we can't get these for love nor money at home." The postie nudged his fellow postie and said, "See, I told you so."

Looking back at my mate he said, "He thought it was part of a grenade!" It was placed back in the box and mailed home. Our next stop too … I travelled back to the UK with Tony.

When we arrived at Kuwait Airport, there was an X-ray machine just before the check-in desk, which I had not seen up until this point in any airport. Thinking we had left the excitement and dramas behind us, Tony placed his bags on the conveyor, as soon as they disappeared inside the X-ray the inspectors started doing cartwheels, jumping up and down pointing!

They asked Tony what the item in his bag was? It was a 0.5-inch drill round as it had pre-punched holes in it and was clearly visible on the monitor. They asked Tony to open up his bag.

On unzipping it, 2 large blue bits became visible, it was one of the French practice bombs that he had broken down to fit into his bag together with the ballast for the bomb, a sort of powdered lead. We heard the Arabic word for 'propellant' mentioned to which Tony said, "It's not propellant."

"We do not care what it is, you are not having it!" was their reply. They asked for his passport and told him to follow them. Wondering if Tony was being interviewed, arrested or getting the rubber glove treatment, after about 10 mins he returned with his passport, items confiscated and onwards with our journey home.

Those last fourteen months were one hell of a rollercoaster ride and I had some of the best times with some unforgettable and memorable experiences.

I worked with and met, some of the best people and I still keep in touch with many of them.

THE OILERS

I was out of the UXO business for some 18 months having tried and failed at business. It wasn't that the business was unsuccessful, just the unscrupulous people I decided to partner with in Cambodia.

I almost ran out of money due to my naivety, so I decided it was time to go back to work. I was getting regular e-mails from a UK company, but none fitted my skill-set. Then I got an e-mail from them saying they needed someone with magnetometer skills and previous Iraq experience. I applied and after them wanting to know my every movement of every day for the past 18 months, I got the job. My medical this time was a self-funded trip to my GP; how things had changed!

I went to the company HQ in London where I met a fellow employee called Tony, on the same project starting at the same time.

A young, really bright lad, almost verging on genius. He was different in many ways as he had never been in the military, he had just completed a qualifying EOD course in Kosovo at great expense, which he passed with flying colours, but he had never been to Iraq. We got on quite well and bounced off each other.

This time we were based in Basra and clearing seismic lines for one of the many oil companies. Seismic lines are a massive grid where either small explosive charges or a large impactor vibrates the ground, this is picked up by sensors and depending on the readings received, they can tell what the rock strata is, and more importantly, if and where there is oil below.

There were the usual bunch of Brits, all ex-Royal Engineers, and equal amounts of people from Eastern Bloc countries, which I didn't expect. I can't be more specific in my detail as I even have trouble with my left and right. 'I was me being me' and already I could sense some bad vibes. Initially I thought there were elements of racism with some of them, right from the beginning, not so much on the skin colour on their part, but I couldn't put my finger on it. In no time at all, a divide appeared, it was like a gaping chasm, it became a real them and us situation, so they ended up with the nickname of 'The Mafia'.

It was a difficult and unpleasant job because of this and I almost hated every day working with most of them.

Due to the great distance we travelled daily, a small secure outpost was built on the actual concession and eventually, we, well all the people on the ground, moved there. It was pretty poorly made, the showers regularly failed to work properly and you either got scalding or freezing cold water at the tiniest movement of the tap, that's even if they worked at all. The electrics were none too safe either and after a rainstorm, someone was electrocuted, thrown some distance to the ground but luckily survived.

As time went on there were elements of the job that I was unfamiliar with but I soon picked them up. The size of the area was quite overwhelming and it took a few weeks to get our bearings. You could spend an hour or so driving round just looking for access to the work site as there were irrigation channels everywhere.

Water wasn't really too much of a problem here as it was previously marsh and there were pockets of water all over the place. I had two managers, one was a Brit, handsome, dashing, chisel-jawed deputy country manager, his words not mine, an outstanding person and manager. (I have to say this as I still work with him with any future pay rises depending on him).

The other one constantly singled me out for all the worst jobs and duties.

The LNs on this job were a hard lot and had seen and received more than their fair share of hardship under Saddam's regime. Almost all of them had lost members of their family. Many had deformed fingers and one of them had a piece of finger missing and had been shot twice, another had half of his ear cut off. They were good hard-working lads and I had a lot of empathy for them but could not even begin to imagine the traumas they had all suffered.

THE HANDOVER (SCREEN GRAB IMAGE)

Work plodded on and slowly large swathes of Iraqi countryside were again free from UXO.

The ordnance we were dealing with was nothing new that I hadn't seen already, only a lot lot less of it, a few bits here and a few bits there. It was still dangerous none the less. I was in charge of the accountancy, sorting the live from the empty ordnance and advising the Iraqi Army what could be safely moved and what not, ready for the final hand-over to them.

One major incident did happen here, well two actually and the next a few months later. It was one November Sunday morning around 7am, I thought I heard my neighbour leave his room as my door moved as his shut, but this was not the case. Within five minutes there was a commotion and shouting in our compound, another roadside bomb had gone off 2km away, killing one of our local security teams and injuring another … this had been meant for us. Not a good day.

We were confined to camp for a week or so before I went on leave. When I left, the Iraqi army escorted us off the concession and it consisted of a number of heavily armed Humvees donated by the Americans.

We didn't stop at any of the checkpoints and we even had several salutes on the way.

While at home, and in light of recent events, I thought to myself, let's be extravagant on leave otherwise what's the point in doing what I'm doing for no reward. So I hired an Aston Martin while I was in the UK.

It was an experience, quite a disappointing one in fact, not as jaw dropping as I thought it would be. I did get the most out of it as I could by sharing the experience and letting most of my close friends take it for a drive themselves.

During another Christmas in Iraq, I couldn't face the disappointment of a poorly cooked Christmas lunch, so I cooked it for everyone.

It went down well; we had roast goose that had been wandering around the compound the day before! There was even Harrods' Christmas pudding that I had picked up from the airport on the way out. We had a bottle of Arrak, traditionally made from grapes and aniseed the night before which was shared between the Brits.

Tony, the youth that came out with me was teetotal, he didn't even drink tea or coffee as he didn't see the point. He wasn't forced at gun point, but almost, to join in the Christmas cheer. Needless to say, he was ricocheting around his room that night.

There was another incident ... although we were all personally armed for our protection, I had heard that some of our internationals had been right up to the north of our site to test out their weapons, which at the time I hadn't. But I thought that as long as we were in a deserted area it wouldn't be a problem. We were in an area where there were a lot of wild boars, and these were often killed by the locals and used as dog food since pork is off the menu in Iraq. One of my managers had said on many occasions that it would be OK to shoot one, as it would supply us with a BBQ, meat and a morale boost.

On the Monday I saw my first boar, when it stood up it was massive. The biggest thing I had ever shot was much smaller, and I just couldn't do it.

In the evening I mentioned this to my manager, and he replied, "I can't believe you didn't shoot it."

On the Wednesday about 10am, I was summoned by my security team and told that the pig had been sighted.

We drove up to where it was, about 150 meters off the road. I spotted it and fleetingly thought to myself, 'this is OK to do'.

I readied my AK47, heart pounding and a 101 thoughts going through my mind of possible consequences, I had been given the go ahead by my manager, so it wouldn't be a problem, only my security team were there and no one else about …

'what if, what if, big BBQ, great for morale …'

So, safety off, I took aim and fired but the shot was high. I'd thought I could do it with one shot and didn't want to draw too much attention with the sound of gun fire.

'Hmm do I fire again'?

I did and caught it in the shoulder, then another shot to try to bring it down; I missed again, it started running off and went behind a large clump of bushes. I reapplied my safety catch and waited to see if it would come out.

When it eventually came out, I took my safety off again but inadvertently put it into automatic fire, oops! Four or five shots were fired and I still missed every shot.

'What do I do'?

The adrenalin was pumping, I had already fired off more shots than I ever intended to but I had wounded it and wanted to end its suffering, so had to finish it off one way or another.

Eighteen shots later (so much for being a sharp shooter!) the pig ended up in a large pool of water, couldn't get out and finally succumbed to the deeper water and died.

After about 10 minutes an official police vehicle pulled up with a police commander in it.

'I'm so, so in the shit now'! I thought.

One of my security team spoke to him in Arabic and I think the conversation went something like, "Ello ello ello, what's been going on here then? I heard some shooting ..."

"The crazy English man wanted to shoot a pig, to eat!"

"To eat?"

"Crazy English man!"

"Did he get it?"

"Eventually, he's a shit shot!"

"Well, tell him not to do it again."

"OK, I will," and he drove off. I was so relieved but didn't know whether to be concerned about the Iraqi officialdom.

We recovered the pig during lunch time. With the aid of a long length of rope and some local boatmen, we managed to eventually get it on the road and into the back of one of the trucks.

Work over, we drove back to camp, the pig was of great interest to everyone and all the cell phone cameras started coming out in force. Soon after our arrival and thanks to our manager, the news had reached London within two hours.

Myself and one of the Fijian security team who had dealt with wild pigs before built a fire to de-hair it, we then butchered it up and put it in a spare freezer.

On the following morning, I was told that I had to get rid of it and was forbidden to eat it. I was devastated that the pig had died in vain and if I had known this would be the outcome, I wouldn't have even contemplated shooting it as it was a sad waste of the pig's life.

Within days I was out of work and on my way back to the UK. I was later told this was intentionally done to get me out and an unqualified mate of his put into my position.

-

Within the first month of arriving back in the UK, my 84-year-old Father was taken ill. My Father was a Jamaican settler who, on the 21st June 1948, arrived on HMT Empire Windrush at Tilbury Docks. It was the first voyage of the calling by the 'Mother Country' to help re-build England after the war.

Sadly, four months after I got home, he passed away. My youngest sister and I were at his bedside, the sun was shining and birds were chirping. Two months later I was in India putting his ashes in the River Ganges.

I think in the greater scheme of things, my dismissal was meant to be, as it allowed me as much time as I needed to do what I had to do.

TWO CANDLES FOR DAD

NEVER SAY NEVER AGAIN

This was the last time I was to work in Iraq but the most important thing for me was to see if I was still employable owing to the swift exit from the last company. The only medical I had this time was a mandatory HIV test at the local Iraqi hospital.

The work, seismic lines again, was for an Iraqi company with an Armenian boss. When I first met him, I thought he was a really nice bloke. He had put a lot of confidence and investment into three new starters - project manager, his deputy, and myself.

There were originally five other expats on the job too but within a few weeks one of them got sick and it was confirmed he had AIDS, so he was immediately removed from the project and he made it as far as Dubai before dying.

My job title was 'Senior Data Analyst'. Not being too 'au-fait' with computers, I had hoped I would pick enough up and learn on the job.

Within the first week we were flown to Germany to be shown how to use the metal-detecting equipment, navigational equipment and analytical software to decipher the data we had collected, as it was a different system from the previous job. What should have been done in a three-week course we did in a week.

"Plug that in there, change this and that, don't touch that Harry, this is set to this and this does that ..."

I thought my head was going to explode! In between all that, yet more info on the job in hand was being discussed, protocols, methodology etc. In the evenings I was going over the information we had been given in the day, trying to make more sense of it.

We then flew back to Iraq. Between the deputy manager and myself we tried in vain to get the equipment up and running. But it was so user-unfriendly and inconsistent in its operation, that after a few days of pushing a wheelbarrow-type contraption up and down the car park and several e-mails back to Germany, we started getting results.

We finally managed to get one piece of equipment up and running. Next, was the vehicle-towed metal detector and it came with a whole new bunch of problems, poorly made equipment with 101 cables going from computers to control boxes and radios connected to the framework of actual detectors. It probably worked great on a football field but not in an oil field in Iraq, with uneven ground, a driver who couldn't drive in a straight line to save his life, and a boy who couldn't quite grasp the concept on how the data was collected for a few weeks, plus stray radio waves and above all ... the heat. No electronic equipment likes the heat; one day I left my watch, with a thermometer outside in the sun for half an hour and it reached 160°F.

On the Sunday, it was off to Abu Dhabi and Sharjah in the United Arab Emirates for a map-making course.

'If I'd been sent on a Mandarin language course it would have made more sense to me and I would have learned much more', I was getting constant headaches because of information overload.

The deputy county manager and my work-aid went home due to a family emergency. I was more or less left with getting all of the non-functioning, multi-disciplined equipment functioning; together with trying to organise the analytical software side and try my hand at cartography, as this is where all the project information had to go through. Even though the project manager had attended the courses with us, he insisted he was only there to make up the numbers and any assistance from him was under duress. He also had his job to do.

Our journey to the work site took about an hour and the site covered an area of over 500 square km and it took ages to get anywhere and find the teams as they were working on different tasks. There were the usual checkpoints, anytime there were obvious internationals in the vehicles there would be extra checks, passports and visas to be inspected and other personal paperwork checked. I did find that if I sat in the back of the vehicle and not say anything then I could pass for a local, which sped up the journey time somewhat.

The journey to the sites passed many de-gassing stations, large flame stacks burning off the gas coming from the established oilfields. This caused so much smoke in the air that sometimes it would completely block out the sun and would make it seem like the cloudiest day in England. The smoke would leave a trail of several miles across the otherwise clear sky.

I couldn't help but consider the environmental impact every time I drove past. There were large lakes of oil in the countryside and on speaking to one of the locals about them he told me that in the past the oil pipes had been broken into and the oil that was smuggled across the border was sold up to $10,000 for each consignment. This had continued for over two years before the practice was stopped, but all the leaked oil had created these huge oil lakes.

DEGASSING AND OIL LAKE

My Father and I never had much of a close loving relationship and I never really discussed with him much of what I did. When I did tell him bits about my adventures at work, I was met with an almost blank face.

With his passing, I felt his presence around me, and to me it seemed for the first time that he could see what I was doing.

I was working late as usual one night and an article was on the BBC about the West Indians coming from Jamaica to England. I was sure it would be interesting as it was part of my heritage.

I thought, 'stop work, take five and watch it'. But within a few minutes I was so exhausted that I fell asleep.

Then I felt a heavy thump on my chest, it was as if my Dad was saying, "Oi, watch this!"

I didn't go back to sleep, that was for sure. So many times working late at night, I would often feel a presence of someone watching over my shoulder and it would bring a wry smile to my face and a real feeling of comfort.

I was working longer and longer hours, in one week it topped 20 hours a day but it was always over 18. I was exhausted. The company owner turned up, not so happy at our lack of progress.

"All you are thinking about is going on leave and eating food in the cook house," he said. We ate hot dog sausages, fried, boiled, chopped and on something they called pizza, for almost a month ... I don't think it was the food on my mind.

Despite being pretty mild mannered, I took umbrage at this and said, "My mind has been 110% on the job for weeks now, I was only eating one meal a day as that's all I had time for, and I haven't even called my daughter for two weeks."

I was not best pleased at the thanks I was being given.

I was sent to another project for a few weeks. This site was around 2km from the Iranian border and was a site where there had been fighting between the two countries, apart from the usual ordnance other remnants left over were countless un-cleared mine fields, rolls and rolls of barbed wire, empty ammunition cans, tank scrapes to help conceal them from a distance and the odd bomb sticking out the ground.

They had the same equipment as us, they too were experiencing difficulties with the equipment and hadn't used most of it for a number of months due to its problematic nature. They dusted down and broke out the vehicle-towed metal detector from storage for my benefit and within two days the connecting arm had snapped off, so they reverted to the wheelbarrow pushed ones.

Whilst I was there, there was a kangaroo-court where they had tried to find ways of dismissing my project manager, but I acted aloof and didn't feel at all happy at what was happening and really didn't want any part of it, but I remained as diplomatic as possible.

The deputy project manager was still at home awaiting a visa to get back in. The project manager was away as he had his leave booked long in advance with plans to go home.

That left two people who had been demoted and were refusing to do anything more than was necessary. A senior EOD tech, a safety coordinator and myself. This was a huge multi-million dollar project with effectively three people running it.

'Argh! When they both left for a week, I was the main man on the project'.

I was out on the ground making sure all was running as smooth as could be, liaising with the client, making quite good maps daily for our staff to work on the ground and as an update for the client, due to my baptism by fire. I was actually getting a buzz out of it, apparently since I started doing the reporting and mapping, inaccuracies went from over 30% to less than 2%. I was quite pleased with what I had accomplished in such a short space of time and to be complemented by such a prestigious client as well.

On one Friday, quite near the end of this 'blood out of a stone' contract and the Muslim holy day which is the day where almost all go to Friday prayers at the mosque, I had a small and welcome break from work.

I had a few hours off and went on a shopping trip to Basra to buy some extortionately priced western food which would make a change from the cheap and nasty goop and weird concoctions we were always being fed by our (in name only) cook at camp.

This was just over an hour away and we were driven into town by one of our locals to The Basra Centre, a large shop by Iraqi standards and sold household goods, food, sweets, toiletries and more. When we arrived we realised it was closed! No one had told us, but it was typical of a Friday.

We wandered across the street to another shop, which was closed too. We waited for our driver to bring our vehicle to us. While we waited, I sat on the high curb looking up and down the almost empty street. It hit me like a brick in the face as to what my current situation was. I was in downtown Basra, in the open, no security, no body armour, with no weapons present. This would have been utterly inconceivable a few years earlier, but there I was.

Having spent over 3 years in Iraq by now and all that had been deeply seated in my psyche was that Iraq was a real dangerous place to be. I didn't know what to think or what to feel ... am I fearful, vulnerable, exposed ... was I in danger? I just looked up and down the street with the same thoughts going over and over in my mind.

We got picked up, drove back to camp empty handed and went back to work. Five months in and almost all the original internationals had left, or they were replaced.

Myself, after not being on the same song page as the new project manager, decided that my reason for being on this project was that I was still employable and didn't need to be there anymore. Within a few days I was back home and shortly to be moving on to pastures new.

WHERE AM I NOW?

The last few years I have been working offshore with ROVs (Remote Operated Vehicles) and on dredging vessels, identifying and disposing of the history of ammunition from the early cannonball, sea mines, air dropped bombs of WWII to practice bombs from the 70s and missiles of the Cold War.

Without the stress of facing the daily bombings and shootings that were and are still going on in Iraq. I guess I can now feel safe. I love my work, for the great people I've met, for the places I have been and things it has allowed me to do.

ACKNOWLEDGEMENTS

To all my EOD brothers and sisters throughout the world, risking your life and limb day in day out, the austere conditions you endure to do the work we love to do, making the world a bit safer for everyone and giving some people a better quality of life.

As ever ... "STAY SAFE."

ABOUT THE AUTHOR

I am the youngest of 5 siblings and was born in the mid-60s in the East End of London to rare (at the time) interracial parents. Leaving London at the age of 2, we moved to a small holding in Wales until my parents divorced 3 years later. From there, my Father, Brother and myself moved to a small-minded racist town still in Wales, with another move in 1977 to Suffolk where I now call home.

I was raised by my Father who while practical, and innovative, he had no interest in aesthetics. So not only being the only mixed-race kid in the town for a few years, I also stood out with homemade jumpers with odd patterns and colours in them.

On leaving school I worked as a kitchen porter at a local hotel before joining the Royal Air Force as an armourer, where I initially worked on the Tornado aircraft and eventually to get my initial training as a bomb disposal #2 operator. After a 6-year stint I was now a civilian with not much call for bomb disposal outside of the forces.

I undertook a few practical positions before spending an interesting and life changing year backpacking around the world where myself and my fellow travellers found ourselves briefly at the mercy of armed Kashmiri militants. Having survived that, for a number of years after this incident I felt almost invincible.

Several positions later I was back with my first passion, working for an EOD company as there was now a call for it due to defence cuts and commercial EOD companies popping up mainly dealing with the risk mitigation of possible unexploded German bombs dropped in London.

Due to personal circumstances, I was offered a position in Iraq which I enthusiastically accepted. The Trash Men of War is my account of this amazing adventure ...